"THERE OUGHTA BE A LAW!..."

...that all small business owners know
how to understand and use
their financial statements.

JIM SCHELL

For distribution information, please call:

Opportunity Knocks
541-318-4650
Bend, Oregon

Printed in the United States of America
ISBN: 0970933517

JIM SCHELL
-ABOUT THE AUTHOR

A graduate of the University of Colorado, Jim Schell has been doing his small business thing for 40 years, the first six years as an employee. Over a 25 year Minneapolis career, Jim bootstrapped four businesses, one of which grew to 200 employees. He is the founder of Opportunity Knocks, a statewide peer problem-solving organization for small business owners in Oregon. Jim has written six books on small business including co-authoring Small Business for Dummies. He currently is down to owning one business but is always on the prowl.

Jim's wife Mary also is the owner of a small business, a Bend-based distribution company with the "sweetest little Balance Sheet east of the Cascades."

Jim has three sons spread strategically across the U.S., so that wherever he goes, a grandchild cannot be far away. He and Mary reside in the hold-on-to-your-hat community of Bend, Oregon, an outdoor playground disguised as a small town nestled dryly in the high dessert just east of the Cascade Mountain range. Two dozen golf courses lurk invitingly nearby, sometimes too invitingly.

Dedicated to the small business owner, our nation's
number one employer. May you enjoy success
beyond your investor's, your creditor's and your
own wildest dreams.

JIM SCHELL

AN INVENTORY OF THE "KLINCHERS" YOU'LL FIND IN THIS BOOK

KLINCHER #1 (See Foreword)
"Once you make the commitment to start your own cabinet business you are no longer a cabinet maker who happens to own a business, you are a business owner who happens to make cabinets."

KLINCHER #2 (See Law #1)
"No one, I repeat no one, can give you conclusive advice on how to manage your business without that person first knowing how to understand and use your financial statements."

KLINCHER #3 (See Law #2)
"The number one service your banker provides is to hold you accountable."

KLINCHER #4 (See Law #3)
"Financial statements can tell you what you did yesterday (P&L's) and where you are today (Balance Sheets) and where you're going to be tomorrow (cash flow projections and Budgets.)"

KLINCHER #5 (See Law #4)
"There is one overriding rule that must be remembered whenever you're dealing with numbers. They are always the most useful when compared to other numbers."

KLINCHER #6 (See Law #5)
"Decrease expenses. Increase Gross Margin. Increase Sales. These are the only three options you have when you want to positively impact your profitability."

KLINCHER #7 (See Law #6)
"If you don't have the cash to pay yesterday's bills and to meet tomorrow's payroll, then your profitability really doesn't matter."

KLINCHER #8 (See Law #7)

"Besides using the Key Indicator Report to manage decisions, its biggest advantage is keeping key employees involved in the direction of the business."

KLINCHER #9 (See Law #8)

"Approximately right now is better than exactly right later on."

KLINCHER #10 (See Law #9)

"A customer is someone who buys your products AND pays his bills within an agreed-upon time."

KLINCHER #11 (See Law #10)

"Inventory is the most dangerous asset of them all!"

KLINCHER #12 (See Law #11)

"When things aren't going the way you would like them to go, trying harder doesn't work. The only thing that <u>does</u> work is to "try differently", i.e. to make a fundamental change in the way you conduct your business."

THERE OUGHTA BE A LAW...

CONTENTS

PREFACE

Several months ago at the frantic telephone request of a local business owner, I dropped in on his business. He needed advice the fellow told me, his retail business was having cash flow problems. Whereupon he, gulp, informed me that he couldn't pay his bills, all $200,000 of them!

I asked to see his financial statements, turned my eyes immediately to his Balance Sheet, and in less time than it takes to say *"wouldyoulikeketchupwithyourfrenchfries,"* I determined this fellow's business was bankrupt. (Easy read, tough call.) As it turned out, so was he. This sad situation had been brewing for the better part of a decade, his business had never been cash flow positive during any of those years and he had kept it alive by feeding it, spoonful by painful spoonful, with his life's savings.

Several months later a similar call, this time a husband and wife business. Same chorus, different verse. Once again, the trusty Balance Sheet told the sordid tale, the problem had been brewing for five years or more. And once more, good old me, rapidly turning into the Grim Reaper of Small Business, is called upon to be the purveyor of bad news.

Hence the notion to write this book.

For starters, such business-failure scenarios are definitely not fun, for me or for my, uh, "customer." (In such cases I volunteer my services.) More importantly however, the events that result from these situations are devastating to the party of the second part. Not only are the economic lives of the owners ruined, in the case of the husband and wife business, 40 employees also lost their jobs. How sad. How wasteful. And how preventable.

Hence the motivation to write this book.

In both cases, had the business owners asked for help from their CPA, or had they talked to a lender or credit officer at their local bank (unfortunately both businesses had been financed by the

1

owner's 401 (k)s hence no business loans were involved), or had the business owner asked for professional help from me or from Jack the Ripper or from any other Tom, Dick or Mary who knew how to read financial statements, these situations could have been prevented. Or – always the best solution of them all - had these business owners known how to understand and use financial statements on their own, these tragic events never would have occurred.

THERE OUGHTA BE A LAW! – YOU CANNOT START A BUSINESS WITHOUT FIRST LEARNING HOW TO UNDERSTAND AND USE YOUR FINANCIAL STATEMENTS! You and every other small business owner should, before you're allowed to ring up your very first sale, be required to attend good old FSU (Financial Statement University), or take a Financial Statement 101 class at your local community college, or find a Financial Statement mentor or consultant or guru. You should be required to do something! Anything.

Hence….this book!

Please digest its contents with care. These are your life's savings we're talking about here.

FOREWORD

Let me guess. I'll bet you believe, I mean truly believe, that your business builds the finest - lets say - cabinets in your community. Maybe your county. Perhaps even your entire state.

Congratulations I say, that's nice. Very nice. Great cabinets are essential to everyone and thus to the overall American economy. Why? Because if we don't have workable cabinets then we can't get our socks out of the drawer in the morning and thus we'll be late to work whereupon our Gross National Product will plummet and the United States economy just might hit the skids. So congratulations on your contribution to our financial well-being. Your great cabinets certainly play a role.

But while great cabinets may have a positive effect on the Gross National Product they won't necessarily have a positive effect on your business. You can make great cabinets until the cows come home but if you don't shovel in more dollars than you shell out your days of making great cabinets will be numbered. So what will happen to our national economy then? Or, more importantly, what will happen to your own personal economy?

You can't tell me for one minute that Mrs. Fields makes the greatest chocolate chip cookies in the U.S. of A. No way, my grandmother, God rest her soul, could make Mrs. Fields look like Tom Thumb when it comes to baking yummy chocolate chip cookies. So can a few hundred other folks I know.

What Mrs. Fields *can* do better than my grandmother and just about everyone else in the world is make a good chocolate cookie *and* run a great business. That's what sets her apart. And that's what will set you apart, too. You run a great business and you won't need to make great cabinets. Kick in however, great cabinets with that great business of yours and what have you got? Why you've got the next Microsoft, or Wal Mart or Mrs. Field's Cookies. Or whatever it is you want your business to look like when it grows up.

3

And what is the number one determinant of running a great business? That's easy, the number one determinant will be the manner in which you manage the fundamentals of its finances, which just happens to be the number one shortcoming of most entrepreneurs and small business owners. Let's face it, who wants to learn about debits and credits and Balance Sheets and Profit and Loss Statements when there are cabinets to be made and customers to be satisfied and employees to be trained?

Why this book?

"THERE OUGHTA BE A LAW!..." is written to open your eyes to the importance of understanding the financial fundamentals that go into building a successful business and to help you use those fundamentals in conducting your day to day business affairs. This book is offered to you by your friendly banker who, believe me, wants you to succeed almost as much as you do. After all, the two of you are most likely joined at the hip in your business in one form or another. Besides, you're part of the same community and communities count!

I work closely with over 50 different small businesses on a monthly basis. I see the good ones, I see the bad ones and I see the in-between ones. And I know the difference between the good ones and the bad ones and the in-between ones and I can tell you this for a fact: "Those folks who own and manage the "good ones" either 1) understand exactly how their numbers work or 2) avail themselves of someone who does.

These then are your two options. Either thoroughly understand the fundamentals of small business finance that you'll find in this book or stay close to someone who does. No, wait a minute, hold your horses, there is one more option, and it is most certainly the best option of them all. That option is to understand the finances of your business yourself *and also* stay close to someone who does. This then is the killer application of them all.

Your grandfather, or maybe even your father, may have owned a business in which he kept his receipts in one Cigar Box and his payables in another Cigar Box and the number of dollars in his checking account measured the success of his business. Sorry folks, but the times have changed and so have the basics of small business. Cigar box accounting has gone the way of the Underwood typewriter and WorldCom's Chief Financial Officer. May it rest its weary head in peace.

The Difference Between a Hero and a Successful Hero

So, Mr. or Mrs. Entrepreneur, whether you're starting a new business or managing an existing one, congratulations on your contribution to the American economy and thanks for the jobs you provide and the mouths you feed and the services your customers enjoy. You are, in my eyes anyway, the economic heroes of this country, in a time when economic heroes are in short supply.

But remember, if you want to be not only a hero but more importantly a *successful* hero, never lose sight of the fact that building cabinets is only a part of what you do, and, you heard it here, it is really not the most important part. What I'm saying here is that **"ONCE YOU MAKE THE COMMITMENT TO START YOUR OWN CABINET BUSINESS YOU ARE NO LONGER A CABINET MAKER WHO HAPPENS TO OWN A BUSINESS, YOU ARE A BUSINESS OWNER WHO HAPPENS TO MAKE CABINETS!"** There's a huge difference!

Thanks for making the commitment to read this book, and I wish you luck both in digesting its contents and in winning the small business game. In the event however, that you don't believe in luck, I suggest you apply the lessons herein. Whereupon you can forget the luck.

LAW #1

YOUR ACCOUNTANT:
MUCH, MUCH MORE THAN A
TAX PREPARER

Before we go any further, you must first recognize one immutable fact about this entrepreneurial career field you have chosen. It is, without a doubt, the loneliest career field of them all. Corporations, non-profit organizations, public entities, governments, all have some kind of internal mentoring, consulting and/or training program established to provide guidance and direction for both their new and veteran managers and employees. Not so for us small business folks. We've embarked on this roller coaster ride alone. When we have a problem we solve it ourselves using the same trusty management tool our entrepreneurial predecessors have relied on for years - good old Trial and Error.

Yes, love our small business as we may, this career field is the loneliest profession of them all. As a result we must constantly be on the lookout for help. After all, whatever problem we are facing today, someone else has faced it before. This much I can assure you: There is nothing new in the world of small business. Everything we consider to be new is really only a variation of something old. Someone has gone before.

The best place to look for that someone to help us avoid our upcoming pitfalls? Enter your friendly Accountant. For purposes of this book we'll call him your Tax Advisor, he could however be a Certified Public Accountant (CPA) or Enrolled Agent (EA.)

Tax Advisors? Come on now, why would I choose such a subject to lead off a book on small business finance? After all, Tax Advisors come at the tail end of the business cycle, after the books have been closed, after the fiscal year is finished. They take those year-end numbers that we have so painfully gathered, run them through their mind-numbing exercises and then hand us some dastardly number that represents a sum that we supposedly owe the Feds and the State. Then they smile, fork over an invoice for services rendered that exceeds the sum of our monthly paycheck plus two month's rent and wave a friendly goodbye until next year.

Well, maybe that's what *your* Tax Advisor is presently doing, but that isn't what he should be doing. After all, your Tax Advisor, is in a unique position. This person is most likely to be the only outsider close enough to your business and your financials to offer you general consulting advice on the direction of your business. He is, as we speak, probably the only person in a position to help you decipher your financial statements and to provide you with meaningful direction.

Please understand this point: **"NO ONE, I REPEAT NO ONE, CAN GIVE YOU CONCLUSIVE ADVICE ON HOW TO MANAGE YOUR BUSINESS WITHOUT THAT PERSON FIRST KNOWING HOW TO UNDERSTAND AND USE YOUR FINANCIAL STATEMENTS."** Financial statements are the first place any professional consultant or turnaround expert worth his salt goes when asked to help a struggling business. The financial statements – assuming of course, that they are correct – always tell the tale and your Tax Advisor is in a key position to interpret that tale.

And what if those financial statements aren't correct? Then this tells a tale of its own. And not a happy tale I should add. As a rule it portends a tale of mismanagement and lack of attention to detail.

Who Is Your Tax Advisor and What should You Expect From Him?

You say your current Tax Advisor doesn't do this kind of general business consulting? Are you sure? Have you asked? Remember, this is your money and your future that is on the line, thus you have good reason to ask. After all your Tax Advisor probably believes that you are (sadly) like most other in dependent-to-a-fault small business owners that he does business with, i.e. you don't want help from anyone. Sure, in a perfect world your Tax Advisor would volunteer to give you the advice you need to steer your business. Unfortunately this isn't a perfect world. Recognize this fact and work around it. Ask for his help!

You say you'd welcome help from your Tax Advisor but he isn't capable of providing the quality consulting help you need? Then the answer is simple, you have the wrong Tax Advisor! I can guarantee you this: there are a number of Tax Advisors in or around your community who are capable of providing the kind of help you need, you simply haven't looked hard enough. Ask the right questions and elevate your expectations to where they belong. (You don't settle for mediocre quality when hiring employees do you? So why should hiring a Tax Advisor be any different?)

OK, so I'll admit that most Tax Advisors, even the good ones, don't know diddly about the cabinet business. But I can tell you this, the good ones do know diddly about interpreting all those numbers on your financial statements and they do know diddly about entering all those numbers on your cash flow projections and they do know diddly about managing receivables and managing inventory and generating your financial statements on time. You see, they have long since learned that small business problems are generic and they've been looking at these same, identical issues for their other small business clients for as many years as they've been counting their beans.

Most Tax Advisors have access to the financial statements of a number of other small business clients. It just may be that he might have another cabinet maker as a client. Or at least another wood fabricator. Or certainly another light manufacturer. Thus he'll have surely have a number of figures to benchmark against your figures (without of course, telling you from whence they came.)

You'll find, once you begin looking for the perfect Tax Advisor (some tips on how to go about this process coming up shortly) that not all Tax Advisors want to do the kind of consulting I'm talking about here. Some simply want to do their number-crunching "compliance" work, i.e. they're content to crank out their numbers and fill out their forms. Which is fine, it's their business and they can run it any way they choose, but these folks are not intended to be the service provider of choice for the savvy, successful entrepreneur. Savvy, successful entrepreneurs need meaning behind the numbers their Tax Advisors provide.

Tips On How To Find the Best Tax Advisor for You

1. When selecting a Tax Advisor, you'll do best to consider one from a small to medium size firm. These folks manage or are involved in small businesses too and can better relate to your business. Plus their fees don't have to finance marble foyers and gurgling waterfalls.

2. Develop a short list of candidates. Talk to other small business owners, your banker, your attorney, your insurance agent. The market knows.

3. Interview your Tax Advisor candidates as if you were interviewing a key employee for a key position. Most will generally allot you 30 free minutes to do so. (Remember, they have but one product to sell. Their time. Learn to respect it!)

4. Ask the following questions of your Tax Advisor candidates:

- How long have you been a Tax Advisor/CPA/EA? What other licenses do you hold?
- Do you have any client businesses similar to mine?
- Who will actually do my work?
- What are your billing rates? How are your fees calculated?
- What can I do to keep my billings to a minimum?
- Do you provide consulting advice? Have you done so for others? Do you have any set consulting programs in place?
- If I were to ask for an annual check up on my business, what are some of the subjects you would review?
- Might I need to upgrade my present accounting system? If so, describe the procedure, the product and the cost.

5. When interviewing candidates, ask for a list of current clients you can contact. Then check those referrals, just as you would a potential employee's.

6. Once you've narrowed your list to two or three candidates, indulge in a breakfast or lunch with your top picks. Besides getting a free lunch (if they don't pick up the tab you've learned a valuable lesson already), you'll get an idea of the synergy that could develop between the two of you. Synergy is always a necessary element of any successful Tax Advisor/client relationship.

When To Use Your Tax Advisor

Once you've located and retained Mr. Wonderful, there are at least two times a year that you absolutely, positively must meet with him and a third time that is optional:

Session #1: Tax Planning and Strategizing: October or early November (if you are on a Jan.1 to Dec. 31 fiscal year, otherwise one or two months before the end of your fiscal year): Review your year-to-date financial statements, estimate your year-end results and make your year-end tax plans. Don't wait until December, do it while you still have plenty of time to make the moves he'll suggest.

Session #2: Annual Check-Up and Physical: Just as you should ask your doctor for a physical checkup every year, so you should do for your business - it has its aches and pains too. Schedule this session as soon as you've generated your year-end financial statements, don't wait until March or April when the financial news is stale. Also remember that the Tax Advising business is a seasonal business and March and April is the heart of THE SEASON. You won't get the quality time you'll need from your Tax Advisor if you get too close to April 15. Ask him to review your year-end financials, both P & L and Balance Sheet. Also have him review your Key Indicators. What is the good news, what is the bad? How is the business progressing compared to the previous year? What danger signals do you see on the horizon?

Session #3: (Optional) Semi-annual Check Up and Follow-up. This session should take place after you've generated your financial statements for the first six months of the fiscal year. You'll need to review the results of the year's annual Check up (Session #2) and see what kind of progress you've made. Or haven't made.

Assuming your Tax Advisor charges $125 per hour, these first two visits will cost you upwards of $300. A small price to pay for such a large potential reward.

My light finally went on...

I must admit, it wasn't too long ago that I was considering putting a contract out for those Tax Advisors who didn't offer unsolicited, business-health advice to small business owners, whether or not the advice was requested. After all, I reasoned, how can they NOT tell you when your Current Ratio has slipped below the 1:1 minimum, when your inventory only turned twice last year or when your Gross Margin came in at ten points below the industry average? How can they NOT tell you that your money would be better invested in T-Bills?

But my light has finally gone on. Unless you've specifically told those folks exactly what you expect of them (kind of like your employees, right?) you're going to get exactly what you ask for. Which is, as my mother used to say, kind of like what the little boy shot at.

Oh yes, for those of you who aren't familiar with the tale my mother was referring to, the little boy shot at nothing. And if you aren't outlining your expectations - for your Tax Advisor and for anyone and everyone else you depend upon - that's what you will be shooting at too.

Tax Advisors are by far your best resource for financial and accounting advice, but they are not the only show in town. There are other possibilities lurking about, if you know where to look. Mentors, Boards of Directors and yes, even consultants are always options to help you wade through the financial issues of managing your business. Also, don't overlook other successful business owners, current or retired. Business owners who, through some unique networking connection, might agree to find the time to help you work through the same problems that they're already had.

Trial and Error has been our management tool of choice for too long. It is high time to replace it with experience. Someone else's.

LAW #2

YOUR BANKER'S NUMBER ONE SERVICE IS NOT RELATED TO MONEY

Let's begin this Law with a question. Paper out. Pencils ready.

"What is the number one service your banker provides?"

Finished? Let me guess, I'll bet your answer had something to do with money, right? Like provides capital. Or makes loans. Or gives away cash to needy entrepreneurs. Something like that?

Sorry, but that wouldn't be my answer. My answer would be: **"THE NUMBER ONE SERVICE YOUR BANKER PROVIDES IS TO HOLD YOU ACCOUNTABLE."** Yep, that's the answer I'd give and I'm sticking to it. Accountability it is.

Let's face it, most of us got into this small business career field because we were drawn to the independence it offers. We liked the freedom, the lack of structure. We've tried it the other way and we made crummy employees. We had all the answers and our bosses had none and besides they were all raving idiots. Whereupon we had to get out of their madhouse and get into our own madhouse – a place where we could at least do things our way.

Which is the American way of doing things and in my opinion the freedom and independence is worth all of the incumbent downsides. However one of the negative results of being the Chief Enchilada is that we end up with no boss of our own and thus no accountability. And we think that's nirvana and in many ways it is but in one way it isn't. Accountability, in the right hands, is good for the soul, as well as for the business.

The message here? Everyone's gotta be accountable to someone.

Accountability? So What's the Big Deal?

Every successful business owner needs a goal to pursue, whether that goal is publicly stated or not. And being the less-than-perfect homo sapiens that we are we need someone to congratulate us when we accomplish our goal and someone to chastise us when we don't. Enter our friendly bankers. They are the only ones who can get away with the chastising part. Our employees can't, and our vendors can't and our spouse probably could but she doesn't understand the extent of whatever it is we have gotten ourselves into this time. Yes, we need accountability in our business life and our banker is the only person in a position to apply it.

You'd better believe that bankers, the good ones anyway, will wield their accountability like a razor-edged sword once they've made the decision to dole out their cash. They'll ask you the tough questions and demand accurate answers and they'll do many of the things that a Board of Directors would otherwise do. After all, they too are likely a significant investor in your business. They have the right to make you accountable and they have long since learned that accountability is good. So lighten up when they tell you need to improve your Current Ratio. They're doing it for your own good.

Not too long ago I worked with a local business owner who had one of the most anemic Balance Sheets you can imagine. The right side of his Balance Sheet was teeming with liabilities, including a mid six-figure loan from a local bank and a dozen or so VISA cards that had long since been maxed out. The harried owner was paying more each year in interest charges than he was taking home. When I asked him what his banker had to say about his long list of high-interest liabilities, he sheepishly told me that the banker wasn't aware of them. The business owner had had the same banker for three years and he had never been asked to explain his Balance Sheet and/or explain his debts. As long as his interest payments kept coming on time, the banker asked no questions.

His banker was doing this owner no favors! To the contrary, he was let off the hook. By the time I was brought in the situation had gone too far, too long. The business was on its last leg and the owner was burned out.

Impressing Your Banker

Alright, so once you've found a banker that will hold you accountable AND give you the money you need, you will want to impress him. Here are several suggestions you can follow to accomplish that:

1. Prepare a three-year pro-forma (projected P & L and Balance Sheet) on an Excel spread sheet. Keep it current, updating the actual results. Meanwhile keep your banker updated on your progress. They'll know you understand financials and they'll know you understand spread sheets and most of all they'll know that you "get it." (Can't handle the technology involved in all that information gathering? Then have your Tax Advisor teach you. Or have him do it.)

2. Call your banker more often than he calls you. Call him with the good news and call him with the bad. Bankers hate surprises, especially those of the bad variety.

3. Follow up your banker's suggestions. Most good bankers keep notes of their meetings, they know that if you don't follow up with your banker, you won't follow up with those other folks who need following-up on a day-to-day basis.

4. Invite your banker to visit your business at least once a year. Let them kick your tires.

5. Face up to the fact that you'll have to personally guarantee your loans. Bankers aren't making an exception of you, that's just the way they do business. You would ask for guarantees too if you were in their shoes.

6. Don't expect your banker to be a venture capitalist. Risk isn't in their vocabulary. They need collateral and they need personal guarantees and they don't do start-ups. They are in business to generate a fair return on their investment at the same time they are protecting your grandmother's CD. They are not in business to take risks. Risks are for risk takers.

Finally, I want to make one thing perfectly clear about bankers. They know more than you think they do about running a business. Much more. OK, so they don't run one themselves, but that usually has to do with their stomach for accepting personal risk, not their knowledge base. Most lending officers, the folks you and I deal with when we want their cash, have a portfolio of a hundred or more small businesses. They know when our Gross Margin isn't what it should be and they know when our payroll is higher than it should be and they know how to read and understand and interpret the minutiae of our financial statements, often better than we do. Like I said earlier, business is generic and they've seen it all. They may not know about manufacturing cabinets, but they know about small business and the folks that conduct it. You and I are nothing new to them.

So what am I saying here? I'm saying that your banker, if a good one, can also serve as your guru and even your mentor. Use him. Take his advice and try his suggestions and let him hold you accountable. And when your banker asks how you are going to improve your receivable collections and you tell him you'll commit to lowering your collection period to 35 days, then, by cracky, do it! He'll be impressed and you'll feel good and best of all, your business will benefit.

And that's how accountability works. Most of us need it, we've got to get it somewhere.

LAW #3

USING YOUR
FINANCIAL STATEMENTS
TO MANAGE YOUR BUSINESS

Let's suppose, just for a moment, that it's the end of the month around your house. It's, argghh, bill paying time again. You gulp down two aspirin, crack open a beer and pull out the monthly stack of bills to be paid, all $4,000 of them. Then you peek in your checkbook and the sad little number in the right hand column totals exactly half of that $4,000. Sorry my friend, but you have a cash flow problem. Just like the big guys.

Now let's suppose, instead of beating the desk and tearing your hair and cursing the IRS like you normally do, you phone a financial advisor and ask for help. Here's what the financial advisor will do:

Step #1: He'll add up your bills and subtract your checkbook balance, just like you did. Eureka, he's created a cash flow statement and determined that you have a cash flow problem! Just like the big guys.

Step #2: Next he'll ask you what bills you're going to have in the upcoming month. Same as last month? Anything new? Then he'll inquire as to what income you expect to receive during that period of time. Same as last month? Anything new? Whereupon he'll subtract your anticipated bills from your anticipated income and determine approximately where you'll be, cash flow wise, a month from now. Eureka, he's created cash flow projections! Just like the big guys.

Step #3: Now that he understands the depth of your problem - both today and tomorrow - he'll inquire as to what you've done to get to this sorry point. Then, after you've shrugged your shoulders and scratched your head and mumbled "I dunno" he'll pull out your checkbook and your VISA statement and your bank statement and begin categorizing your monthly expenses. (Hopefully you don't conduct your personal affairs with an ATM machine. Please, please say you don't!) Then once he's got your monthly expenses categorized – mortgage, utilities, insurance, health, entertainment, etc. – he'll review your income (revenue) from the past month. Once he's finished tabulating your income with your expenses subtracted below he'll have a nice little piece of paper that points out exactly how many bucks you took in last month as opposed to how many you shelled out. Eureka, he's created a profit and loss statement! Just like the big guys.

Step #4: Now that he knows the depth of your problem and now that he knows why the problem occurred it is time to determine a temporary solution. (Note the key word "temporary" here, the permanent solution, unless your last name is Buffet or Kennedy or Gates and you can continue Eternal Deficit Financing, is to take in more dough than you shell out). To make this determination Mr. Financial Advisor will need to know what outside resources you have that will allow you to generate the cash you'll need in order to settle your bills. Whereupon, after he's asked the right questions he'll have a tidy little worksheet that will list all the assets you own, including those that can be readily turned into cash (current assets) and those that can't (fixed assets). Then he'll list on the other side of his tidy little worksheet the liabilities you owe – outstanding bills and car payments and mortgages and such. And assuming your assets are more than your liabilities he'll determine your net worth. Eureka, he's created a Balance Sheet. Just like the big guys.

Now at last Mr. Financial Adviser understands the depth of your problem (you owe $2,000), and he knows the cause of your problem (you lost $2,500 on the slots in Vegas) and he knows the "temporary" solution to your problem (you'll need to cash in a CD) and he knows the long term solution to your problem (no more Las Vegas or get a hefty raise or find a night job).

Business 101

And this folks, is Home Business #101 and it is also Biz Business #101. This example illustrates exactly why you need financial statements. **FINANCIAL STATEMENTS TELL YOU WHAT YOU DID YESTERDAY (P&L'S) AND WHERE YOU ARE TODAY (BALANCE SHEETS) AND WHERE YOU'RE GOING TO BE TOMORROW (CASH FLOW PROJECTIONS AND BUDGETS.)** And frankly, you should be using financial statements at home as well as in your business and personally, this old timer can't imagine life without either one.

No, I'm not one of those anal, conservative, number crunching types. Neither am I an actuary or a CPA or a lawyer. I'm a hip-shooting, gun-slinging full-speed-ahead entrepreneur, just like you. It's just that I've learned that I need a minimum of order in my life and more than a minimum in my business. A lesson I've learned the hard way.

Using Your Financials To Manage Your Business

A wise old sage once made the statement that *"if you can't measure it you can't manage it."* Well whoever that wise old sage was, he or she was certainly right. Management (of resources) is what financial statements are all about. Thus financials are all about measuring what you do so that you can learn how to manage what you do, be it at your home or be it your business.

That wise old sage has obviously learned, if you don't manage your business (and your life), it will manage you.

Besides, if you aren't using your financial statements to manage your business, you're wasting your money. I know of a company for instance - $3 million in sales – that employs a $40,000 per year controller. Tack on another $10,000 or so for miscellaneous accounting-related expenses (computer, software, supplies, employee benefits, etc.) and we're talking $50,000 a year to, in a large part, generate accurate interim financial statements. Now I ask you, what kind of business decision is it to shell out fifty grand a year to generate data that you don't use? Or at least to use that data only to pay your taxes? If you think that's a sound decision then I've got a bridge you might be interested in.

The situation described above applies to every business. Whether or not you have $3 million in sales, you do have costs associated with generating your financials. In addition to a bookkeeper or a controller you probably have a software accounting program (Quick Books, Business Works, Peach Tree etc.) that is programmed to crank out your financials at the push of a button. Thus you have both access to data you can use and costs associated with collecting that data, similar to the $3 million company mentioned above. It seems to me you gotta learn how to use it. I mean, where's the downside?

Furthermore, I swear, I can tell within five minutes of looking at a business's financial statements, what the owner's personal strengths and weaknesses are. I can tell whether the owner is neat and orderly - his financial statements will be up to date and his expense, asset and liability accounts will be culled and current. I can tell if the guy has a spending problem – a review of his P & L expenses will provide that information. I can tell if he has a follow-up problem - his accounts receivable compared to his monthly sales will tell that story. I can tell if he has an attention-to-detail problem – the size of his inventory compared to his monthly sales will be the tattletale here. I can tell if he has a problem managing his employees - his payroll as a percentage of his sales will be the key indicator here. I can tell if he has a partying problem - the trusty entertainment expense account tells no lies. It's a fact, a business owner's financial statements are better than any ink blot test or personality profile when it comes to getting inside a fellow's business soul. No wonder we small business owners are so reluctant to let outside folks peek at ours.

Keeping Score

One final point on financial statements in particular and "numbers" in general. While I know that the collection of data, and the numbers that go along with it, conjures visions of green eye-shades and musty ledgers and dimly lit rooms to many of us, nothing could be further from the truth. Think about it, numbers are nothing more than records of someone's activities, activities that come as the result of things you and I do. Just as the Yankee Stadium scoreboard displays how many overpaid baseball players have crossed home plate at any given time, so it is with your version of a scoreboard – your P & L, Balance Sheet and Cash Flow Projections. You sell a cabinet, that activity turns into a number on the P & L. You buy a lathe, the cost turns into a number on the Balance Sheet. You buy a box of cigars for the guy who buys your cabinets in quantities and that figure shows up on your P & L. Every number has a home.

I can honestly say that I know of no successful business people today who don't understand how numbers work in their business environment. Not a one.

LAW #4

UNDERSTANDING YOUR BALANCE SHEET: THE MOST TELLTALE FINANCIAL STATEMENT OF THEM ALL

A s I write this book, the explosion, implosion and erosion of once mighty WorldCom is playing out, another in a long line of tawdry Fortune 500 failures. Every day a new set of abuses comes to light. The slant of the WorldCom story that is of interest to us small business owners however is this: a well respected analyst had been loudly touting the stock in advance of its decline, focusing, as stock touts are prone to do, on the *future potential* of the company. The real issue was however, that WorldCom didn't have a strong enough Balance Sheet to get past today, let alone enjoy its *future potential*. In other words, those guys couldn't pay their bills!

The moral of the story: Tomorrow's never come if you can't get past today.

This lesson applies to Mom's Diner as well as to WorldCom. If I've heard this lament once from small business owners, I've heard it a gazillion times: *If only I could start over again I'd control the universe,."* Or maybe *"If only I could get caught up on my bills I'd knock my competitor's socks off."* Or perhaps *"If only I could get the bank loan paid off I could buy a second home in the Bahamas."* Sorry folks, but *"if onlies"* don't count in the world of business, be it small business or Fortune 500. Your Balance Sheet doesn't care what might have been.

As I've mentioned before, whenever I'm called to assist a troubled small business the first place I look is their Balance Sheet. The Balance Sheet is a snapshot of a company's financial position at any point in time, you can crank out a Balance Sheet any day of the month and it has immediate relevance. It measures your overall financial health TODAY, right now, at this very instant. It shows what your company owns – it's assets; it shows what your company owes – its liabilities; and it shows what's left over – it's net worth. And it shows everything in between, to the eye of the discerning reader anyway.

Let's take a look at a Sample Balance Sheet and see how it works.

RUBBER DUCKEY INC.
BALANCE SHEET AS OF DEC. 31, 2002

	Current Year	Prior Year
Current Assets:		
Cash	$25,000	$20,000
Accounts Receivable	100,000	80,000
Inventory	125,000	75,000
Total Current Assets	$250,000	$175,000
Fixed Assets:		
Furniture & Fixtures	50,000	45,000
Equipment	150,000	125,000
Total Fixed Assets	200,000	170,000
TOTAL ASSETS	**$450,000**	**$345,000**
Current Liabilities		
Accounts Payable	75,000	70,000
VISA Payable	25,000	20,000
Total Current Liabilities	100,000	90,000
Long Term Liabilities		
Uncle Charley Note Payable	150,000	160,000
President's Note Payable	50,000	50,000
Total Long Term Liabilities	200,000	210,000
TOTAL LIABILITIES	300,000	300,000
Net Worth	150,000	45,000
Total Liabilities and Net Worth	**$450,000**	**$345,000**

Taking a Physical of Your Business

OK, so here's your exercise for today. Let's pretend you called me and asked for advice on the health of your company. We're talking a physical here I hope, not an autopsy. After all, I'm a doctor, not a coroner.

So haul out your Balance Sheet and let's wade through the following exercises together. Let's review some of the key figures and develop several key ratios and indicators from those figures. (You'll need your Balance Sheet from a year ago and your most recent Profit and Loss Statement along side you as well. We'll use the Rubber Duckey Balance Sheet as an example to help us understand how the numbers shake out.)

We will incidentally, discuss in more detail the use and application of ratios and percentages in Chapter 7 when we get into explaining how to develop your own Key Indicator report. Suffice it to say here that ratios and percentages provide a tool by which to measure the relationships between the financial statement numbers your business generates, thereby allowing you to compare them to previous numbers as well as to numbers that similar businesses generate.

Oh yes, one more thing before we get started with your physical. I'm assuming here that your accounting system is generating accurate and trustworthy numbers. If it isn't, we have a much bigger problem. The thermometer is busted. I can't even take your temperature.

- **Exercise #1: Current Ratio computation.** Let's first compute your Current Ratio (a ratio that measure's your business's "liquidity") by dividing Current Assets by Current Liabilities on your Balance Sheet. For your information, this is the first place bankers look, what's happening here is that they are determining the liquidity of your business. Think about it, if you have more Current Assets (assets that can be turned into cash within 30 days) than Current Liabilities (debts that must be paid within 30 days) you can cover any 30 day calls on cash that might occur. If the resulting ratio is say, 2 to 1 or higher (current assets over current liabilities) most banker folks would consider you to have a healthy current ratio. If the ratio is in the neighborhood of 1 to 1 you are perched on the perimeter of your danger zone. If it is less than 1 to 1, take the phone off the hook and get to work. You've got some catching up to do.

Using Rubber Duckey's Balance Sheet as an example, it's Current Ratio is a healthy 2.5 to 1 ($250,000 divided by $100,000.) Another positive note for the Rubber Duckey folks is trend. The Current Ratio last year was 1.94 to 1. ($175,000 divided by $90,000.)

After completing this exercise I'll know how immediate any cash flow problem you have may be. I'll also have a good idea as to how much time you have to solve your problems.

- **Exercise #2: Debt to Equity review.** This is the ratio of what you owe (debt) to what you own (equity). In other words, if your equity (a.k.a. net worth) is more than you owe then your Debt to Equity ratio will be in excess of 1 to 1. This quick exercise gives the reader a snapshot view of who it is that can call the ultimate shots in your business – the bank, the creditors, your Uncle Charlie, or you.

Rubber Duckey's debt to equity ratio is 2 to 1, the $300,000 in liabilities divided by the $150,000 in net worth (equity.) We're seeing a nice trend here as well, prior year's Debt to Equity ratio was 6.6 to 1. ($300,000 divided by $45,000.)

After completing this exercise I will know who *really* owns the company. And who is lurking in the background, keeping a wary eye on you.

- **Exercise #3: Accounts Receivable review:** Your Accounts Receivable are, unless you are running a cash business and there aren't any, an integral part of your Current Assets. Accounts Receivable represent cash-in-waiting, they are the next best thing to cash and should be treated as such.

First I need to know if your Accounts Receivable are collectable and I need to know how quickly your customers pay. I'll look at your P & L to determine the dollar amount of last month's sales. Now back to the Accounts Receivable balance on the Balance Sheet, are the two numbers in the same ball park? If, for instance, your receivables are $200,000 and your monthly sales $100,000 this tells me you probably have a collection problem – you've got two months of sales in your receivables which means that either your customers are paying in 60 days (too slow!) or you have some extremely slow payers in your midst. Or worse, you have a festering lump of ancient receivables that aren't going to be collected at all. Whereupon, if you have to write off some of those receivables, you're going to adversely affect your Current Ratio by doing so. A quick look at your Accounts Receivable aging – an updated list of all those folks who owe you money including the "age" of their invoices - will tell the ultimate tale. (You do have an up-to-date aging available, I hope?)

After completing this exercise I will now have an idea of the relative collectability of your receivables and of the health and well being of your Current Ratio. I will also have an idea of how well your office and its systems and controls are managed. Good office systems and controls usually beget good accounts receivable.

• **Exercise #4: Inventory review:** Another key element of your Balance Sheet (unless you're a service provider and don't carry inventory for sale or resale), is Inventory. Since Inventory, like Accounts Receivable, is a Current Asset, it is an important element of the Current Ratio computation as well. I'll glance at your monthly sales figure again from your

P & L, and compare that to the dollar amount of your Inventory in order to determine whether or not the business has too much or too little inventory.

This is a more difficult exercise than the accounts receivable exercise, because the Balance Sheet shows inventory at cost while the sales figure from the P & L includes the addition of Profit (hopefully there's plenty of it) and any Cost of Goods Sold that you might have. I've got to make a quick mental calculation to adjust the inventory figure on your Balance Sheet to include that profit and Cost of Goods Sold figure. Once I've made that mental calculation I will be able to estimate approximately how many month's sales you have in inventory and how many times a year you're turning your inventory.

Let's say you have $100,000 in sales and $200,000 in inventory. Upon asking the right questions I'll determine that you mark up your inventory by say, 100 percent to include profit and cost of goods sold. Thus that Inventory, when converted to sales dollars is really $400,000, which means you have four months of sales in your inventory. Which also means you're turning your inventory three times a year.

In essence, an inventory turn of 10 or more means you're turning your inventory almost once a month. A turn of 6 means you're turning it every two months. A turn of two indicates twice a year. Are these turns good or bad? You'll have to consult your inventory trade association for that answer. Every industry is different.

Once I've completed this exercise I will have an idea of how well your business manages its inventory compared to other businesses in your industry. I'll know approximately how many times your inventory turns. Or translated – I'll know how well you understand the role of inventory (after all, its just another very dangerous form of cash) and how well you manage it. I'll also have a good idea as to how well you manage details, since inventory is one of the most important "details" of them all.

• **Exercise #5: Liability review:** Next I'll review your Accounts Payable aging (similar to your Accounts Receivable Aging, this report details your creditors and the "age" of the monies due them), your notes payable and any outsize liabilities that you might have. How about that note to Uncle Charley, do you really have to pay it back? If so, when? What is the interest rate? What is Charley's collateral? How about that note to yourself (President's Note Payable), do you need to pay that back in order to pay your taxes next year?

I'll also look to see if you are financing your business with credit cards. If you are, this will tell me something about your credit rating and something about your interest expense and something about your ability to find money elsewhere. While I am fully aware that many start-ups use credit card debt to finance their early growth, if your company is more than two years old and you're still juggling credit cards then something is amiss. We'll need to explore alternatives.

Once I've completed this exercise I'll have a strong indication of your credit rating and how easy, or hard, it is for you to find money and how you manage your relationships with vendors and creditors and how you are perceived by the credit community.

• **Exercise #6: Comparison to Prior Year:** First an important point to remember: **THERE IS ONE OVERRIDING RULE THAT MUST BE REMEMBERED WHENEVER YOU'RE DEALING WITH NUMBERS. THEY ARE ALWAYS THE MOST USEFUL WHEN COMPARED TO OTHER NUMBERS.** With that overriding rule in mind it is now time to haul out your Balance Sheet from one year ago. We need to know not only where *you are,* but also where you've *been.*

Imagine for instance, that today your Current Ratio is say, 1.2 to 1. Is that good, or is it bad? My response would be that it's good if, a year ago it was .8 to 1. On the other hand it is bad if, a year ago, it was 2 to 1. It's trend that counts here, which is why you need yesterday's numbers.

Look at Rubber Duckey's Current Ratio compared to Prior Year, this is definitely a figure that is trending in the right direction. Ditto with its Debt to Equity Ratio. The only disturbing trend I can see on the Rubber Duckey Balance Sheet is its inventory. Inventory increased by 66% over the prior year (from $75,000 to $125,000.) I'd need some answers as to why the big increase.

...Back to Your Business

OK, now back to *your* business. Are your receivables cleaner (i.e. has your % over 60 days gone down?) this year than they were a year ago? Is your inventory leaner? Is your credit card debt up or down? How about your liabilities as a whole? And, of course, your net worth, where is it compared to a year ago? Ah, so many questions, so little time. In order to answer them all, hopefully you'll understand why it is necessary that we brush the dust off of yesterday's Balance Sheet and compare the numbers.

While we're on the subject of comparing numbers, here's a tip that you should adopt the day you design the format for your first financial statement. Always include at least two columns of numbers on your P & L and Balance Sheet and preferably three. The first column should be your Current Year results, the second column should be your Prior Year results and the Third Column, assuming that you prepare an annual budget, should include your budgeted numbers. Using this multi-columnar format you'll always have at least one and sometimes two numbers to use for comparison purposes.

Once you've concluded the exercise of comparing today's numbers to yesterday's numbers you'll know officially where your company's financial condition, and your business as a whole, is trending. Is it trending up, trending down or holding steady. In other words, is your business growing or dying?

Now that we've determined the state of your business's solvency it's time to take a look at what it is that is determining its trend. What's causing it to trend up, trend down or hold steady and what changes do you need to make to change any negative trends? This story will be told by your Profit and Loss Statement.

LAW #5

USING YOUR PROFIT AND LOSS STATEMENT TO MANAGE YOUR BUSINESS'S DIRECTION

While the Balance Sheet is a difficult financial statement to read, the Profit and Loss Statement is, at first glance anyway, quite simple. Heck, you start at the top of the statement with your sales (Sales, or Revenues), then, working down, you subtract whatever those sales cost (Cost of Goods Sold), then also subtract all the other expenses that aren't directly related to your products or services (Overhead) and what's left over is profitability. How linear. How easy. How quick.

Most entrepreneurs feel that they are capable of reading the Profit and Loss Statement and thus are inclined to believe that they understand it. They get lured into this complacency by the relative simplicity and ease of reading the P & L. But reading it is one thing, understanding it is another and using it as a tool to manage the business is still another.

While it is true that the P & L is an easy statement to read, it is not until you begin using the P & L to actually manage the direction of you business, will you really learn to understand what it is and what it isn't. It is NOT a document simply to be used to determine your bottom-line profitability and then pay your taxes. It IS a document to be used to manage the direction of your business.

A Word About Format and Selecting Key Percentages

Before we get into using the Profit and Loss statement as a management tool, let's go back to "format" for a minute, as discussed in the previous chapter. In addition to the Prior Year and Budget columns, the P & L requires still another column - a column entitled "% of sales." This column will appear to the right of each of the Year To Date, Prior Year and Budget columns, and will allow the reader to quickly determine what percent of the total sales each line item constitutes. Sure, the page now becomes much busier and harder to read, but remember we're looking to create a management tool here, not a children's book.

Let's take a look at what an abbreviated Profit and Loss Statement might look like for a small manufacturing company:

RUBBER DUCKEY INC.
PROFIT AND LOSS STATEMENT FOR
THE YEAR ENDING DEC. 31, 2002

	Current Year	% of Sales	Prior Year	% of Sales
Sales	$1,000,000	100	$800,000	100
Cost of Goods Sold				
Raw Materials	125,000	10	95,000	9.4
Direct Labor (Salaries)	350,000	35	300,000	37.5
Cost of Goods Solid	475,000	47.5	395,000	49.3
Gross Profit	525,000	52.5	405,000	50.7
General & Administrative Expenses				
Depreciation	25,000	2.5	20,000	2.5
Rent	75,000	7.5	75,000	9.4
Office & Admin. Salaries	150,000	15	125,000	15.6
All that other stuff	125,000	12.5	110,000	13.7
Total Expenses	375,000	37.5	330,000	41.2
Pre-Tax Profit	$100,000	10	$75,000	9.4

While every number and percentage will have meaning to you, the President of Rubber Duckey Inc., there are several that are more important than others. Several of those key percentages include:

- **Profitability Compared to Prior Year:** Rubber Duckey earned $100,000 this year, compared to $75,000 the prior year. In terms of real dollars, this is certainly a meaningful increase, wouldn't you agree?

More importantly however, Rubber Duckey returned 10% on sales this year ($100,000 profit on sales of $1,000,000), compared to 9.4% the prior year. Another solid increase. This incidentally, means that for every dollar the company sold, it made a dime.

We've discovered a reassuring trend with this example. Rubber Duckey's profitability is increasing, both in real dollars and in percentage of sales. Can the same be said of your business?

- **Gross Margin:** This is always the figure I look for next, after glancing at the net income figure at the bottom of the page. Gross Margin is the percentage of Gross Profit that you've made on sales *after* deducting the Cost of Goods Sold but *before* deducting your General and Administrative Expenses. Hence the term *Gross* Margin.

To be able to understand the relevancy of your Gross Margin percentage, every business owner should know exactly what the industry Gross Margin standard is for the product or service he is providing. For instance I recently worked with a light manufacturing company who's Gross Margin on his P & L was 22%. Meanwhile after checking with the fellow's trade association I learned that the industry standard was 37%. Since the sales of this company were $2,000,000 at the time, this owner was giving away 15 percentage points (the difference between 22% and 37%) on those sales, or

$300,000 per year! Ouch, how many of us can afford to give away that kind of money?

If you're using your P & L simply to measure your profitability and to pay your taxes, then the pre-tax net profit figure at the bottom of the page will be the first and last place you will look. If however, you're using the P & L to manage the direction of your business, then bottom line profitability will still be number one followed closely by Gross Margin. This is because it won't take you long to learn: The greatest opportunity to make positive changes in your profitability usually lies in Gross Margin.

• **Overhead as a Percentage of Sales:** Overhead is represented by the total of all the "General and Administrative Expenses," or in the case of Rubber Duckey, $375,000. Since this figure is 37.5% of sales, it represents Rubber Duckey's ability to manage it's overhead expenses. In this case the 37.5% figure shows an improving trend over the 41.2% figure of last year.

Theoretically at least, as your company grows you too, similar to Rubber Duckey, should be able to operate more efficiently, i.e. the percentage of your total General and Administrative Expenses as a percentage of Sales should decrease. If this isn't happening with your company, contrary to what your increasing sales figures are telling you, you may not really be growing at all.

Most sophisticated companies will also divide their expenses into "departments"; i.e. Finance and Administration, Sales and Marketing, Operations/Production, etc. Such divisions will allow you to determine, and compare to industry averages, the percentage of every sales dollar spent on department.

- **Salaries as a Percentage of Sales:** Salaries are usually the single largest individual line item on the P & L, whether they are those that are included in the Cost of Goods Sold section of the P & L or those under General and Administrative expenses. You can quickly spot trends in the amount of salaries paid by comparing the percentages from one period to the next. In the Rubber Duckey example, both of the Salary accounts are trending down.

- **Your Largest Expense Line Items as a Percentage of Sales:** After looking at the categories mentioned above, I'll next scan the individual line items within the General & Administrative Expense category to determine where the biggest numbers are hiding – and hence the biggest opportunities to make a difference. Then I'll determine the trend of those line items by comparing percentages between Year to Date and Prior Year.

You say your entertainment expense has risen from 2% to 2.8 % of total sales? Better start sitting in the back of the plane. Telephone expenses up? How many cell phones have you handed out and what are they being used for? Utilities up? Who's responsible for setting the thermostat and turning off the lights at night?

Affecting The Direction of Your Business's Trend

Now that you understand the basics of how to read a P & L, it's time to give me a call again. Me, your trusty, reliable and grossly underpaid financial consultant. Let's see if we can positively influence your business's trend and, in the process, positively impact it's profitability. So pull out your own P & L, complete with (at least) Prior Year comparisons and with the % of sales columns filled out.

Before we dive in however, you must first understand one principle if you desire to become more profitable. There are only three ways to go about it and they come in the following order: 1) Decrease Expenses, 2) Increase Gross Margin and 3) Increase Sales.

- **Step One: DECREASE EXPENSES.** Why should I head for your expenses first? Because they're the easiest of the three categories to affect and because Ben Franklin was right, a penny saved IS a penny earned. Save $100 on your telephone bill and that $100 drops straight to the bottom line. It does not pass GO and it does not go to jail. Not so by, say, adding $100 to your Sales. Sure, you may add that $100 to sales but meanwhile what happens to your line? Maybe, just maybe, you add ten bucks to it, but then too, maybe you don't. It all depends on what you are selling and how much you mark up whatever you're selling and who pays the freight and whether you get paid or not and, well, you get the point. Increased sales don't always lead to increased profits.

Do not, I repeat, do not make the mistake of overlooking expenses as the first place to go when you're set on changing your current business trend. Do not overlook expenses simply because there may be some conflict involved in making the necessary changes, i.e. cutting salaries, laying employees off, changing insurance vendors or asking for discounts. Do not overlook expenses simply because it is a plodding, laborious and bleary eyed exercise. Do not overlook expenses simply because they aren't as much fun as creating sales – which, I'll admit, they aren't.

Alright, since you're digging into expenses, let's interject a word about "budgeting." I suggest you not only begin budgeting, but further I recommend you learn how to "zero base" budget your expenses. Zero-basing consists of making the assumption that your expenses are *zero* and then starting from that point and adding back whatever it is you need do add back. As opposed to what most of us do when budgeting expenses – we simply tack on a logical inflation figure, say 4%, to last year's expenses. Your phone bill last year was $1,000? Then zap, let's budget $1,040 this year and move on. Ho hum, no fuss, no muss.

Sure, zero-basing your expenses takes more time, but once you've zero-based the first time it will be much easier the following year. Then you'll have a template. You'll also determine in the process of zero-basing – and I guarantee it - how easy it can be to positively impact profitability and you'll likely find yourself zero-basing specific line item expenses in the middle of the year. Be careful however, you could become such a fan of this zero-basing stuff that you could morph into an accountant.

• **Step Two: Increase Gross Margin.** Gross Margin can be positively impacted three ways: 1) By increasing your prices, 2) by lowering your cost of raw materials or 3) by increasing your production efficiency.

Pricing is always the easiest to change. You say you think you'll sell 10,000 widgets this year at $4.50 each? Then bump the price a quarter to $4.75 and you'll drop another $2,500 to your bottom line. Simple, quick and usually quite easy, assuming the market will bear the increase. You get the same kind of results here that you get by cutting expenses - the amount of the price increase drops straight to the bottom line.

The second key element of Gross Margin is raw material cost. You'll need to review the prices you're paying your vendors to improve this figure. Is your company getting big enough to demand better prices from your vendors? You'll never know unless you ask. (Try doing business with Wal Mart sometime if you want to see examples of how the Big Boys use clout to get price concessions from their vendors.)

The third element of Gross Margin is production efficiency. You can measure this by looking at your labor within the Cost of Goods Sold category as expressed as a percentage of sales. Has the percentage decreased in the last year? Then congratulations, you have become more efficient.

- **Step Three: Increase Sales.** At last, the fun part. It's about time.

Unfortunately, most entrepreneurs will turn first to sales when times get tough. You say your business is losing money? Then hey, I've got it! Let's throw some more sales at the problem. So what happens? You add more sales to an already inefficient organization and your inefficiency increases and you lose even more money.

The key point here? The organization comes *first,* then the sales.

Let's face it, we small business folks are hung up on sales. How's business, we ask another small business owner. Great, the guy responds, his sales were up 20%. Wow, you think, he's one up on me, my sales were up only 15%. Never mind that the fellow lost 5% on every dollar of sales, you aren't about to hear about that.

I'll admit that sales are fun and a good juicy sale will always bring out the goose bumps and it feels really, really good when you land that juicy one but remember, it's bottom-line profitability that counts. No, wait a minute, it's really cash in your checking account that counts, but we'll talk more about that later. In the meantime I beg, plead and beseech of you if you want to make it to the big time, get off this sales kick and onto the profitability kick. This is one area where our Fortune 500 cousins have it all over us, at least they understand that it's earnings that drive a business, not sales.

The Role of Training

OK, so exactly how do you increase your sales? Well it isn't always by adding more products, and it isn't always by adding more sales people and it isn't always by expanding territories. No, the best way to increase sales is by increasing

TRAINING. That's right, by taking the resources you have now and making them better. Those "resources" include your sales force and your customer service folks and most of all, the people who manage them. That's probably you and maybe your sales manager, if you're company is large enough to have one.

Please remember that "sales" is a skill, not an art. Most of us think of a sales person in terms of a list of predisposed personality traits; i.e. friendly, gregarious, good talker, goal driven, to name a few. If someone we interview possesses those outward traits then, by God, she must be a salesperson, let's hire her before she gets hired by someone else! But wait, hold on just one minute, like I said earlier sales is a skill. How much training has your interviewee had is a better question to ask, especially if you aren't going to offer her any yourself. For sales, like any other skill, can be honed and sharpened, and training is the best way to accomplish that. I'll take a trained professional salesperson any day over a gregarious, story-telling extrovert.

Unfortunately most small business owners aren't chomping at the bit to budget their hard earned dollars to training. That's because we view training as an expense, not as the investment it really is. Meanwhile our Fortune 500 cousins are training their employees, especially their sales ones, by the boatload. One company I know trains their entry-level sales people for six months, then several more times in the first year as they gain experience.

A Word About Benchmarking

Here's a suggestion on how to use another valuable tool for comparing your P & L to yet another group of figures. This tool is known as benchmarking. Webster defines the word *benchmark* as "a standard by which something can be measured or judged." Most trade associations, and yours hopefully will be no exception, have collected from other businesses in your industry an array of benchmarked figures for every line item on the Profit and Loss statement. As a result they have, in effect, created one common business model for the industry. Give your trade association a call, maybe you'll get those benchmarked figures for free, maybe you'll have to pay a slight fee, but you'll find them fascinating reference material, as you line up the industry standard business model against your own.

Is your gross margin in line with industry standards? Are your General and Administrative Expenses too high? How about salaries as a percentage of sales? Compare your Return on Sales (R.O.S), sales per employee, entertainment as a percentage of sales, you name it and you can compare it to a benchmark. And then you can do something about it.

Here's a tip on how to find benchmarks within your industry or SIC code: go to www.rmahq.com. This is the web site for Risk Management Association, formerly known as Robert Morris and Associates. Click on "Annual Statement Studies" and there you will find the opportunity to download financial comparisons for just about any SIC code. This web site will even help you define the ratios and percentages they provide. Yes, there is a cost for the service ($59), log on and make the determination whether the information is worth the cost. (My advice: It is.)

There you have it, folks a P & L primer on how to positively affect profitability. **DECREASE EXPENSES. INCREASE GROSS MARGIN. INCREASE SALES. THESE ARE THE ONLY THREE OPTIONS YOU HAVE WHEN YOU WANT TO POSITIVELY IMPACT YOUR PROFITABILITY.** Attack them in that order, and then, when you're finished, start all over and attack them again.

Profitability is a never-ending process.

LAW #6

UNDERSTANDING
AND FORECASTING,
CASH FLOW

In February of this year I ran into a friend of mine at a Chamber of Commerce meeting. After exchanging pleasantries, I tossed her the old "How's business?" question. A character flaw of mine I suppose, but I can't help it. I've been doing this small business thing too long. Besides, I cared.

"It's wonderful!" she replied and her body language told me she meant it. "I just received last year's financial statements this week."

"Tell me more," I said.

"My sales were up 25%," she said proudly. "And I know what you're thinking Jim, but my profits were up too. 15%!"

"That *is* wonderful," I agreed. I knew she had had problems in the past, I was happy to hear she had solved her problems, although a red flag had gone up with that last statement. While her profits had increased by 15%, they weren't keeping up with her 25% increase in sales. In other words, sales were growing faster than profits, which means there was a leak somewhere.

"One problem however," she said, as if reading my mind. "I'm having more trouble paying my bills this year than last."

The Difference Between Profits and Cash

A few well placed questions and her story came together. Before

I explain the details, there is an old business axiom that applies to this situation. Maybe you've heard it?

"Profits are what you pay taxes on, Cash is what you take home."

Sound familiar?

What this axiom means is that "profit" is an accounting term while "cash" is that hard, green stuff that resides in your cash register and in your checking account. There is a big difference in the two, as my friend was learning the hard way. **"IF YOU DON'T HAVE ENOUGH CASH TO PAY YESTERDAY'S BILLS AND TO MEET TOMORROW'S PAYROLL, THEN YOUR PROFITABILITY REALLY DOESN'T MATTER."** Cash is the fuel that runs your business, while profitability is an accounting term used to settle your tax bill.

Cash flow, quite simply, describes the flow of money (cash, checks, electronic debits and credits) in and out of your business. It is, in short, your checkbook, except that your checkbook only tells you what has happened to your cash, it doesn't tell you why, it doesn't tell you where it is heading and it doesn't help you to arrive at any solutions.

The Three Great Suckers of Cash

My friend with the cash flow problem owns a light manufacturing company, replete with small business's three Great Suckers of Cash: Inventory, Accounts Receivable and Equipment. Great Suckers of Cash? By that I mean those three sneaky Balance Sheet items that suck cash out of a business like those leeches sucked the blood out of Humphrey Bogart in African Queen. (Am I dating myself here?)

Those three Great Suckers of Cash have two things in common. 1) When you fund them they require cash and 2) When you incur them they don't affect profitability, which is why they are called sneaky. They're hiding from your P & L.

What happened to my friend's cash? It turned out: 1) She had increased her inventory significantly during the course of the year in order to satisfy her 25% increase in sales and the new customers that came with it. Funding inventory requires cash. 2) Her accounts receivable had also increased by 25% because it had no other choice as it kept pace with the 25% increase in sales. Funding accounts receivable requires cash. 3) She had purchased a goodly amount of computer equipment in order to keep her systems and controls on track with her increased sales. Funding capital expenditures requires cash. True to form, all three transactions sucked cash out of her business and none of the three affected her P & L.

This story paints a classic picture of how a profitable business can literally grow itself into trouble. If you're in a business where the three Great Suckers of cash are alive and well and if your profits don't keep up with your sales increase, this could happen to you.

I can tell you this: Most successful businesses I know, I mean the really, truly successful ones, project cash flow. They don't want to be caught like my friend with her checking account bare, their owners have learned that cash and profitability don't necessarily run hand in hand. They've also learned that while they can manage the operations of their business using their P & L and Balance Sheet, they need a third tool to manage their cash. Enter the rarified world of Cash Flow Projections.

Projecting Cash Flow

Cash Flow Projections do exactly what they say. They project your future cash flow needs, just as budget projections project your future profitability. They give you a peek into the future, and if that peek shows that you're going to be short of cash by July, then you've got to do something about it in June. Or before.

In essence, Cash Flow Projections are designed to predict what will happen to your checkbook within a given period of time.

What will your bank balance be two months from now? What position will you be in to pay your bills on time? Will you have more cash than you need? Will you have less?

Could my friend have done something about her cash flow problem if she had been projecting her cash flow and known a cash crunch was coming? The answer is an unqualified yes, she could have postponed her capital expenditures. She could have leased the equipment instead of purchasing it. She could have made the decision to maintain her inventory at a lower level, or she could have promoted low-priced sales on her inventory in order to move it, thus decreasing her need for cash. She could have offered cash discounts to customers to speed up their payment or worked her slow-paying accounts receivable harder in order to free up the cash required to fund those receivables. There are a myriad of things a business owner can do to generate cash if you know in advance that it's needed.

I am giving you an overview of cash flow projecting in these pages, however space doesn't allow me to devise a system that will work for you. I strongly suggest that you invest a few hundred bucks by asking your accountant to help you install a Cash Flow Projection system for your business. If your accountant is a small business veteran, this will not be the first time he's been asked to do so. (If he's incapable of setting one up, see Law #1). In the process of developing your own Cash Flow Projections not only will you generate numbers that will aid you in running your business you'll also learn everything you need to know about the ebb and flow of that hard, green stuff that is the lifeblood of your business.

In the process of teeing you up to generate your own Cash Flow Projections, your accountant will give you the option of preparing your projections for one day out, one week out, one month out, one year out, or any combination thereof. Predictions for longer time periods are likely to be fuzzier and less accurate than your predictions for shorter time periods and besides, cash changes too fast. I recommend that you make your cash flow projections for at least six months out, and then update them at least once every month, always remaining six months out. That way you'll spot problem periods earlier and be able to adjust to them more quickly.

Although it's true that most start-up and early stage small businesses will keep their cash flow projections in their head and will not go the trouble of generating written Cash Flow Projections, it is life-or-death important that every small business owner understand the concept behind measuring cash flow. No matter how small or uncomplicated your business happens to be, cash will always be king.

LAW #7

CREATING
YOUR
KEY INDICATORS

A Key Indicator Report is, well, a report detailing your key financial indicators. (Catchy name, huh?) Key Indicators are those numbers, ratios or percentages that you deem to be the most important measurements of your business. You'll select those key indicators yourself, usually 8 to 10 key numbers that represent percentages or ratios that are of particular interest to you, and then have your bookkeeper or controller include the resultant report along with your monthly Financial Statement package.

Yes, these Key Indicators can change from year to year, as your focus changes and as your problem areas ebb and flow. You'll need to review the list annually and add and cull as your little heart desires. Nothing is sacred with the Key Indicators you select although there are a number of them that are obviously more important than others. I would include Sales, Gross Margin, Inventory, Receivables, Current Ratio and Debt to Equity in those more important numbers.

"BESIDES USING THE KEY INDICATOR REPORT TO MANAGE DECISIONS, ITS BIGGEST ADVANTAGE IS KEEPING KEY EMPLOYEES INVOLVED IN THE DIRECTION OF THE BUSINESS. " After all, your employees don't have to know how to read financial statements in order to understand the Key Indicators, all they have to do is understand the individual Key Indicators themselves. Thus the report is really one giant scorecard. Like, say, in baseball, but instead of showing Earned Runs, Home Runs and Strikeouts or whatever the baseball manager wants it to know, the Key Indicator Report shows Return on Sales and Gross Margin and Inventory turn or whatever the business manager wants to know.

The best way to describe a Key Indicator Report is to show you one. So coming up, one sample Key Indicator Report of Rubber Duckey Inc., followed by what might be my commentary if I were running this Duckey little company:

RUBBER DUCKEY INC.
KEY INDICATOR REPORT FOR
THE MONTH OF APRIL, 2002

	Current Year	Prior Year
Profit for April	$14,000	$9,000
R.O.S. – Year to Date	8.5%	6.3%
Sales for the Month	$155,000	$132,000
Web Site Sales	24,000	5,000
Current Ratio	1.8 to 1	1.6 to 1
Debt to Equity	.8 to 1	1 to 1
Inventory Dollars	$198,000	$190,000
Accounts Receivable	$185,000	$130,000
% Receivables over 60 days	12%	3%
Salaries & Wages as a % of Sales	22%	23%
Freight In	$3,500	$5,400

Deciphering the Key Indicator Report

Following is what I, the esteemed and wise President of Rubber Duckey Inc., might have to say to my employees as we review the Key Indicator Report together:

- **Profit for April:** "Good job, folks. Our R.O.S. (Return on Sales) for April of this year was 9% ($14,000 divided by $155,000) compared to last year's 6.8% ($9,000 divided by $132,000.) Thus we continue our trend of becoming more efficient at turning a sales dollar into a profit dollar."

- **R.O.S. Year to Date:** Ditto above

- **Sales for the Month:** "Nice job, sales department. Our sales in April were up 17%!"

- **Web Site Sales:** "It's easy to see where most of our sales increase came from. The Web. Is this a blip or is it going to be a continuing trend? Should we throw some more marketing dollars at our web site? Do we need to spend some redesign dollars on our site? How can we continue to leverage this new direction?"

- **Current Ratio:** "And the beat goes on, chalk up another month of continuing improvement for our Current Ratio. Whooooeee folks, our banker is going to love us again this month. Is this cool or what, watching this ratio continue to improve!"

- **Debt to Equity:** Ditto above. Plus "our creditors can now claim ownership of a slightly smaller portion of our company than they could a year ago. Which is, I should add, just fine with both of us."

- **Inventory Dollars:** "We sold more dollars this year than last on less inventory. That's a great trend, and our cash flow will be the biggest benefactor. Along with the folks in the shipping and receiving department who have to handle the inventory we don't sell."

- **Accounts Receivable:** "Ooops, what's going on here? We have significantly more dollars in Receivables than we do in April's sales. Meanwhile, look at last year's figures, you can see we had approximately one month's sales in our receivables. Which is what it should be if we were collecting our receivables in 30 days. Helen, what's happening here?"

- **% Receivables over 60 days:** "Aha, we've just identified the A/R culprit, we've got a customer or two who is stringing us out. Who are the culprits Helen? What is being done to get them back within terms? Do I need to get involved?"

- **Salaries and wages as a % of Sales:** "Good trend here folks, the improvement in this Key Indicator has been going on for six months now. Our decision at the beginning of the year to become more aware of this expense category is paying off. We've cut down on our overtime and are, judging by our continuing R.O.S. improvement, not losing any efficiency as a result."

- **Freight In:** "We set out at the beginning of the year to make a serious impact on this account, we all agreed we've been spending too much on bringing our inventory in every year. A good job by Charlie in purchasing, he's been controlling our inventory releases and investigating shipping options better." (Note: This Key Indicator category will likely change at the end of the year and be replaced by another one that will be identified as the new fiscal year's number one candidate for cost cutting.)

And that folks, gives you a rough idea as to how you can use the Key Indicator Report as a management tool. It gives feedback to those who are affecting the numbers at the same time it is publicly stroking those who deserve the accolades and imparting a slight slap on the back of the hand to those who don't. We're talking Management 101 here."

LAW #8

GETTING YOUR
FINANCIAL STATEMENTS
OUT ON TIME

As you might expect, the wise old sage of small business also has an axiom to share on this topic of financial statement timing. It's no coincidence by the way, that this wise old sage seems to have an axiom for just about everything we small business folks do. The fellow has long since learned that small business problems are generic. He knows that it makes no difference what business or industry you're in, every problem you have is one that someone else has. Or has had. Be it marketing problems, employee problems, accounting problems, government regulation problems or cruising-the-web-during-working-hour problems, you've seen one, you've seen 'em all.

But I digress. Back to the wise old sage and his axiom on the subject of the timing of financial statements. **"APPROXIMATELY RIGHT NOW IS BETTER THAN EXACTLY RIGHT LATER ON"** the old fellow states. And I couldn't agree more.

What the wise old sage is saying here is that the quicker you can generate your month-ending, quarterly-ending and year-ending financial statements the better off your company will be. Numbers, ratios and percentages, not unlike bananas, get stale with age. Quite simply, it's easier to deal with numbers that are a week old than it is to deal with those that are three weeks old.

Every Day Matters

Let's suppose for instance, that your P & L regurgitates the fact that your Gross Margin came in at 25% last month, when it typically comes in at 35%. This 10% discrepancy is known as "Margin Shrink", and it means you've got a leak, in this case a serious leak, somewhere in the bowels of your company. Employee theft? Outsider theft? Billing problems? Shipping and receiving problems? Pricing problems? There are a variety of reasons that could be responsible for such a sizable discrepancy, you've got to find out why. And you've got to find out now.

So what's the big rush? The big rush is that every day that goes by the trail gets colder. Plus every day that goes by without the problem being corrected, the losses mount. Assuming you find that the numbers are accurate, i.e. that this isn't an accounting problem and you *really are* suffering from a case of acute Margin Shrink, then suddenly the heat from the problem intensifies. Now you're not only looking at Margin Shrink, you're looking at Profit Shrink. And Cash Shrink. We're talking real money here.

Most small businesses I know generate their monthly financial statements somewhere between the 15th and 20th of the following month. This folks, is too late! You should be kicking them out by no later than the 10th of the month and, if you are willing to make one slight adjustment to the process, you can have them out even sooner. That adjustment? Don't wait for your bank statement to arrive, never mind reconciling it to your checkbook. Assume the checkbook is correct and make whatever assumptions are necessary and crank out your financials. Now! Then, when the bank statement arrives, if there are small corrections to be made, you can make the necessary adjustments to your financials. Hence the sage's "approximately right" advice.

Your bookkeeper, controller or CFO will likely squawk about this "approximately right" philosophy. After all, most folks who make their living juggling numbers are fans of "exactly right", and well they should be. They don't like going back and adjusting numbers and they don't like explaining adjustments and mistakes. But your job, in this case anyway, is to overcome their objections. You need those figures to manage your business today. Tomorrow's too late, a couple of minor adjustments pale in importance.

There are Fortune 500 companies with billions of dollars in annual sales who can generate their "approximately right" financial statements within a matter of four or five calendar days following the end of the month. If the big guys can do it, so can you.

LAW #9

STAY ON TOP
OF YOUR
RECEIVABLES

As re you aware that you and your banker have something
in common? That's right, you are both in the money
lending business. The difference of course is that your banker
does it professionally and usually makes a profit on each
transaction. Meanwhile most of us small business owners don't
do it professionally and none of us make money on each
transaction. Thus the term Net 30 days really means "30 days of
interest-free loans."

When a customer buys our product and says "charge it", then
poof!, whether we admit it or not we are in the interest-free
money lending business. After all, the customer has our widget
in his pocket and we don't have his money in ours. Which means
a good deal for him. And maybe a good deal for us if 1) we've
made a profit on the sale and 2) he pays on time. All of which
means that collecting the monies due us is an integral part of the
business cycle. Wait a minute, did I say integral? I meant critical.
As in the difference between succeeding and failing.

Oh, the irony of it all! We lionize our sales people when they
make The Big Sale. But The Big Sale doesn't do our company
one iota of good unless the Big Collection is not far behind. In
fact I've seen more than one The Big Sale lead to The Big Failure
when The Big Cash doesn't follow The Big Sale within a reasonable
amount of time.

Someone must be the Collection Queen

Every successful business needs someone dedicated to the collection of its receivables. In the early stages of your business that someone is usually you. In the later, mature stages that responsibility may be delegated to a bookkeeper, controller or Chief Financial Officer. Whoever that delagee happens to be, he or she must be passionate about collecting monies due the business; first politely following up, then relentlessly hounding, and finally hauling the deadbeats to court.

Many of us love to recite the old "the customer is always right" mantra. OK, that mantra sounds like a good one to me, but before we give the customer our firstborn, we must first define the word "customer. **"A CUSTOMER IS SOMEONE WHO BUYS YOUR PRODUCTS <u>AND</u> PAYS THEIR BILLS WITHIN AN AGREED-UPON TIME."** In other words, no cash, no customer!

After all, accounts receivable are really our cash in someone else's hands and cash is what keeps the doors open. Nobody had better mess with our cash.

Tips on Managing Your Receivables

Now that we understand the importance of converting those receivables into cash, here is a collection of tips designed to help you improve the process:

- **What gets measured gets attention:** Outstanding receivables should be aged (a listing itemizing the status and age of every outstanding receivable) at least once a month. This aging list should sit on either the boss's or the Collection Queen's desk, a constant reminder of who it is that's in possession of the company's cash. Procedures should be in place for every level of outstanding receivable over 30 days – say a phone reminder at 40 days, another at 50 days, a fomal letter at 60 days, a call from the boss at 90 days and then a collection service letter at 120 followed up by the collection agency itself at 150 days. Or whatever order you determine, just make sure the procedure you establish is cast in stone.

• **Check Credit:** You can bet that your banker checked your credit before he lent you the bank's cash, the same was probably true with your professional vendors. Remember, the granting of credit is a privilege. Grant your credit with care.

• **Establish Terms:** No sale should be made without first agreeing on credit terms. Terms should work for both parties but remember, when a customer wants you to carry his receivables for long periods of time, that's your signature on the bank's guarantee. The structure of terms must first work for you.

• **Use a Standard Credit Application:** Design and use a credit application. Look at some of those you've filled out for your vendors and select the one you like best. Every customer should have a credit "app" on file.

• **Evaluate all Credit Applicants:** Ask yourself these three questions before approving a credit application. Does this applicant have the ability to pay? Has he indicated by his past actions a willingness to pay on time? Can you make a reasonable profit on the account? If the answer to any of these questions is no, cede the customer to your competition and move on.

• **Sales Contract:** Design a boilerplate Sales Contract, one that provides the legalese you need to collect your monies in court. Outline everything from payment terms to late payment charges to collection procedures. Officially signed Sales Contracts denote professionalism, and potential deadbeats will usually pay the professionals first.

- **Ask for a Financial Statement:** Don't be afraid to ask for a financial statement before shipping a first-time customer.

- **Up-front money:** When in doubt with a first-time customer, or when a customer needs your products before you're able to complete a credit check, ask for money up front. Failing that, COD is AOK.

- **The older the receivable the less likely to pay:** Don't wait until your receivables are over 90 days to kick in your collection procedure. The sooner you pick up the slow-pays the better.

- **Today doesn't mean forever:** A customer's ability to pay on time changes, as the fortunes of his company changes. Don't brand a slow-pay a slow-pay-forever, rather track his year-to-year progress and make your credit decisions based on his latest performance.

- **Use a collection agency only as a last resort:** Collection agencies are expensive (up to 50% of the receivable). Also, collection agencies are not known for their good manners when dealing with deadbeats, you can usually kiss that customer goodbye.

- **No pay, no ship:** Don't ship to ongoing customers who consistently don't pay on time. After all, your good vendors wouldn't ship to you if you are a career slow-pay. In those cases where you determine that you absolutely, positively, must have the slow-pay's business, be sure to build the cost of carrying the receivables into the sales price.

Finally, I honestly believe that I can walk into your business and quickly determine exactly how professionally it is being managed by asking to look at your Accounts Receivable Aging. If your Aging is quickly produced and is kept in a conspicuous location, if it is neat and orderly and shows signs that someone is actively working it, and if whoever it is that is responsible for it is hovering nearby anxious to explain why Acme Wood Supply has $1,000 in the over 60-day column, then I know your receivables are in good hands. If all of this isn't enough and you want to ratchet this company up still another notch, have that Aging reveal that the company's total receivable dollars approximate the dollar amount of the prior month's sales and that the percentage of A/R dollars over 60 days is 5% or less. Now, in addition to knowing that you manage your business professionally, I'll also know that you understand the role of collecting receivables as it applies to cash flow.

The proof, as they say, is in the Aging.

LAW #10

MANAGE YOUR INVENTORY
OR
IT WILL MANAGE YOU

Are you familiar with the term "asset lending"? Or how about "asset-based lending?" For those of you who aren't familiar with either of the two, these two synonymous terms describe a lending technique that bankers use. The terms describe a transaction whereby the bank uses your business's assets as collateral for a loan. The two kinds of assets most often employed in this type of lending are accounts receivable and inventory.

There's a very interesting difference between those two assets. Typically the bank will lend you an amount equal to 80% to 85% of your accounts receivable dollars but only 40% to 50% (if you're lucky!) of your inventory dollars. So why the difference? The difference is because the bankers are aware that, in the likelihood that you should encounter the Fickle Fairy of Tough Times and they would end up owning your assets, they could probably convert 80% to 85% of your receivable dollars into cash but only 40% to 50% of your inventory dollars.

Yes sir, those bankers have learned the lesson that we grizzled small-business veterans have taught them so many times over the past century or so: **"INVENTORY IS THE MOST DANGEROUS ASSET OF THEM ALL."**

Inventory: The Greatest Killer Asset of Them All

Personally I prefer diamondback rattlesnakes to inventory. Diamondback rattlesnakes are Barbie Dolls compared to inventory. At least you can hear the rattlesnake coming, you can see it as it prepares to strike, and you can beat it to death with a stick.

Not so with inventory. Inventory is the greatest cash sucking, profit draining, killer asset of them all. It just sits on our shelves and collects dust. And interest. And as it sits there it gets older, and yellower and deadlier until its detail-despising owner finally discovers that all of his cash is tied up in shelf after shelf of dust-ridden, obsolete inventory and he has nothing but a motley collection of obsolete widgets left over to pay the bills. Whereupon the creditors move in and the employees move out and all those dusty, obsolete widgets bring the house down.

So what do I really think about inventory? I think that there is money to be made with inventory for those detail-oriented folks among us who are comfortable taking great risks. For the rest of the world I think Russian roulette offers better odds.

Sam Walton had to be the greatest attention-to-detail business owner of them all. Personally I believe that Wal Mart, Sam's company, above all of the other things it does right, manages its inventory better than any other business in the world. They ship and receive and store and distribute their inventory like it is made of gold, which in effect, it is.

Tips on handling inventory

You say that, despite my not-so-subtle warning, you are either going to start an inventory-related business or already have? OK, don't say I didn't warn you, but here are a collection of tips (garnered the hard way, for I am a recovering inventory addict) to help you manage your inventory properly:

• **Take Frequent Physicals:** Are you aware that the accuracy of your Gross Margin figure on your P & L cannot be validated as accurate until you've taken a physical inventory? That's right, in those months, or quarters, when you don't take a physical inventory, your Gross Margin, and thus the bottom line on your P & L, is only an guesstimate. Which means you're taking a chance trusting your numbers in those months. Your reported profit just might be a loss!

If, for instance, an employee begins walking off with your most expensive widgets in June and continues to do so throughout the summer and fall and if you don't take a physical inventory until December 31, then you won't have any idea your inventory has been shrinking until the middle of January, when your financial statements are completed. Or at least the shrinkage won't show up in your numbers, unless, that is, your thief is considerate enough to leave an accounting entry behind. (A debit to Theft and a credit to Inventory.)

The best inventory-managing small business I know takes monthly, that's right monthly, physical inventories. It helps that this company is a wholesaler and doesn't have to close its doors to conduct its inventory, and sure, it takes three employees the better part of a day to count the stuff. But when the P & Ls come out a week after the end of the month the owner knows that they are absolutely, positively correct.

As a result of such exactness the owner of the above-described company recently traced a transaction that had been billed incorrectly during the prior month because she had learned immediately of the resultant margin shrinkage. Imagine the same scenario if her inventories had been six months apart.

My recommendation? Monthly inventories if you can pull them off. Quarterly inventories otherwise.

- **Track the Turn:** Inventory Turn is a number that represents the frequency with which inventory "turns over" and is arrived at by dividing the cost of goods sold (from the P & L) by the year's average inventory (the year's beginning inventory plus the current inventory divided by 2). The higher the Inventory Turn, the more sales dollars the business has in relation to the size of its inventory. See Law #4, Exercise 4 for more on this subject.

- **Utilize the Necessary Software:** An accurate and smooth MIS and paperwork flow is the number one key to handling inventory. Most entry level accounting systems aren't capable of delivering a professional inventory tracking system. Quick Books for instance, might be sufficient for accounting for a retailer's inventory but won't do the job for the manufacturer who needs to track work in progress. An upgrade to Quick Books Pro or to Business Work may be in your cards. Is growth on your mind? Remember that it takes the better part of a year from the time you begin investigating a new system until it is up and running smoothly. Don't wait until your current system is gasping it's last breath before you begin planning the upgrade.

- **Make it a Priority:** If you don't assume direct accountability for inventory yourself, at least make it your personal priority to oversee progress or failure in the goals that you establish. If your employees know that your eyes are glued to inventory levels and to inventory turn, then inventory awareness will become a part of your company's culture.

- **Divided It Falls:** Divide your inventory into small, manageable pieces, allowing for easier tracking and quicker reference. This will also make your inventory lists more user friendly, especially for the folks who have to sell it.

Then get involved in setting mini-goals for those manageable pieces. Identify your most-wanted-to-dump inventory and make heroes of the folks who sell it.

• **Man the Battle Stations:** Make sure there are good employees at the inventory-handling corners: receiving and shipping. Train those employees thoroughly, not only on their own duties but on related bookkeeping functions as well. Most inventory shrinkage problems can be identified, traced and resolved at the bookkeeping level.

• **Take The Hit When It Occurs**: Most bankers I know don't like inventory hits (write-downs) that accumulate but aren't taken, especially when they are serving as the bank's collateral. Sure, inventory write-downs can ruin the current financials, but don't postpone taking the painful ones. Postponing them may rescue the current P & L, but the pain will compound when the truth comes out.

• **Hit the Delete Key:** And finally, when in doubt, cancel the stuff. Your vendors might scream now, but it's a better option than eating it later.

There is some good news on the subject of inventory. The opportunities to improve profitability by the efficient handling of it are boundless. Inventory isn't gray, like marketing, or steeped in hypothesis, like sales. It is there to touch and feel and count, and the impact of inventory exchanged for cash is instantaneous. And oh, so pleasurable.

And one final piece of good news, if you are into the handling of inventory. You won't have me to compete with.

LAW #11

ONE MORE THING
BEFORE WE
PART COMPANY

Let's suppose, just for a moment, that you've encountered a Law or two in this book that has struck a resounding chord. Aha, you've chortled, smashing the table with your fist, this Law makes sense. By golly, I think I'll do something about it.

Now you and I know that you wouldn't be an entrepreneur if you weren't disposed to "doing something about it", which means I'm confident that you will at least *try* to do something about it. But just exactly what will you do? Will you make a commitment to simply try harder, or will you make a commitment to institute a fundamental change in the way you do business.

Here it comes, are you ready? Drum roll, please....

"WHEN THINGS AREN'T GOING THE WAY YOU WOULD LIKE THEM TO GO, TRYING HARDER DOESN'T WORK. THE ONLY THING THAT <u>DOES</u> WORK IS TO 'TRY DIFFERENTLY', I.E. TO MAKE A FUNDAMENTAL CHANGE IN THE WAY YOU CONDUCT YOUR BUSINESS."

We're Muckers, Diggers and Bulldogs

I see this trying-harder syndrome so often with entrepreneurs. We're muckers, we're diggers, we're bulldogs. Whenever we get backed into the corner we grit our teeth and hitch up our pants and by God we work harder. And then harder. After all, that's

71

what got us here in the first place, if we have to scrounge another ten hours out of the week, then so be it, our home life will pay. And yet, there will come a time in the life of our business, when trying harder simply doesn't work anymore. It isn't enough. We need to try something new, something different. Something smarter, not harder.

And so, in your case, in the case of understanding and implementing one or a few or all of the preceding Laws, I would suggest to you, Mr. Mucker, Mrs. Digger, and Mr. and Mrs. Bulldog, that trying harder probably won't be enough. You will need to make a fundamental change in the way you conduct your business. You will need to implement something different. You will need to work smarter, not harder.

Changing Your Financial Ways

Here are a select few of the many options you might want to consider in order to make a Fundamental Change in the way you manage the financial aspects of your business:

- **Upgrade your Bookkeeper:** The bookkeeper you have now may not be capable of projecting cash flow or deciphering your Balance Sheet or giving you advice on collecting your receivables. You have two choices: 1) Train her or 2) Replace her. To replace her will probably cost you another $7,000 per year in salary to upgrade the position (unless she's presently being overpaid), not to mention the cost of training. Meanwhile training your existing bookkeeper will cost appreciably less, but you've got to be sure going in that the training will take root.

- **Hire a Controller:** Maybe your business has reached the point where you need to hire a Controller, the next step up from a good bookkeeper. You'll have the same choices as recited above, either train your upgraded bookkeeper to become a controller or replace her. Tack on at least another $5,000 or so a year in annual salary over the price of a good bookkeeper.

- **Hire a CFO:** You say you already have a controller? Then this is the next step, hire a CFO with a CPA or similar designation. A capable CFO can do it all including working with the bank and even, hallelujah, overseeing most of those mind-numbing Human Resource issues. Tack on another $15,000 a year over the cost of a Controller.

- **Find a Financial Mentor:** Preferably your Tax Advisor, but there may be others out there who qualify. Budget $2,500 or so a year and then schedule your mentor at the end of every month to review your financials and make financial recommendations and give you a taste of accountability.

- **Upgrade Yourself:** There are plenty of courses delving more in depth into the Rules we've talked about in this book. You'll find them on the web or at your local community college or university. Certainly it will take time and yes, time is money, but so is misdirection. If you're going to get serious about taking your business to the next level, upgrading yourself is the most obvious place to start. Anyway, if you want to take your business to the next level you'll have to do this upgrading sometime, sooner is always better than later.

Well folks, thanks for your attention to this book. As you have probably determined, I am an inveterate fan of the kind of people who start and run their own businesses. I truly want every one of you to succeed and I'm hurt and offended when you don't. Plus I don't want any more eleventh hour phone calls.

I would enjoy hearing your review of this book. Feel free to e-mail me at smallbiz5@aol.com and please identify on the subject line of your e-mail either the word "compliment" or "criticism." (My delete-key finger is itchy and I don't handle criticism well.)

Good luck and good business to you all!

Jim Schell